THE GOLDEN YEARS

1964

text: David Sandison, Arthur Davis

design: Paul Kurzeja

SIENA

196

Welcome to The Golden Years and the hurly-burly, helter-skelter of events - great and small - which made 1964 a truly memorable time in which to live. It was, as ever, differently memorable for different people. For Nikita Khrushchev, on holiday while his enemies and rivals plotted and muttered in the summer heat of Moscow, it would mean the end of the line and an unplanned retirement. For Lyndon B Johnson, handed the torch of leadership by horrific events on the streets of Dallas in November 1963, the year would prove memorable for his success in proving himself worthy of retaining that torch in his own right, and for steering through the legislation which John F Kennedy had begun so that America's black citizens could enjoy a level playing-field in the game of life.

It was a memorable year, too, for Nelson Mandela, the South African leader sentenced to a life behind bars for attempting to fight the dread apartheid system. Jomo Kenyatta had also lived behind bars during his fight for Kenya's freedom - but he saw out 1964 as President of an independent nation. America's teenagers got wise to a phenomenon which had swept all before it in Britain and Europe

in 1963 - Beatlemania. As US teens took John, Paul, George and Ringo to their collective bosom, they little knew just how great a flood of other British talent was about to swamp their shores.

The Tokyo Olympics proved especially memorable for Ethiopia's marathon marvel Abebe Bikila, and for New Zealander Peter Snell, but the rest of us could only marvel as the world's most gifted young people really did push themselves to go higher, faster and stronger.

Enjoy this trip back in time. And, please, try not to say, 'Was it really all that long ago?' It was only yesterday.

Pope Paul Visits The Holy Land

MID-WAY THROUGH his historic three day 'peace pilgrimage' to The Holy Land, Pope Paul VI today reinforced his message of unity and reconciliation when he met with the head of the Eastern Orthodox Church, which had separated from Rome during the first millennium.

Pope Paul and Patriarch Athenagoras - who had flown to Jerusalem from Rhodes specifically for the meeting - were the first leaders of their respective churches to meet since the 15th Century. With combined worldwide 'flocks' of nearly 1 billion people, it was, in Pope Paul's view, appropriate that they two leaders should finally meet in the country where Christ had founded his church and been crucified.

After the historical meeting, the Pope moved on to Nazareth, celebrating mass at a place he called 'the school of the Gospel' - the Grotto of the Annunciation, his progress slowed by the vast crowds which packed the route and overwhelmed security men in their efforts to get close to the pontiff.

Alan Ladd, The Big Little Star, Dies

It's hard to comprehend just why Alan Ladd - who died today at the age of 51 - became one of Hollywood's most bankable stars in the 1940s and 1950s, but the facts speak for themselves. After close on 10 years as a workmanlike actor who could be relied on to remember his lines and not bump into the furniture, Ladd got his big break in 1942 when he played a cold-eyed killer in *This Gun For Hire*. From then on his agent had to fight off the producers and directors. There were many who believed Ladd should have won an Oscar for his 1953 classic *Shane*, but were amazed when he even failed to win a nomination.

Despite being physically tiny and of limited emotional range, Ladd became one of those rare performers whose fan appeal far exceeded his abilities. An alcoholic by the early 1960s, he made his last screen appearance in *The Carpetbaggers* and died from a lethal mixture of drink and sedatives.

JANUARY 17

Albert And 'Arold Top UK TV Ratings

Britain had taken two unlikely heroes to its heart in the past year or so, and a new series of half-hour shows had opened 1964 by shooting straight to No 1 in the UK television ratings with an astonishing 26 million viewers - that's about half the entire population!

Albert and Harold were *Steptoe and Son,* a pair of disreputable scrapyard dealers developed from an original 30-minute one-off playlet by its authors, Alan Simpson and Ray Galton. Wilfred Brambell played the grubby, cantankerous and shifty father, and Harry H Corbett his often rebellious, pretentious and inevitably frustrated son.

Steptoe and Son would give BBC TV a huge hit for three years before it closed in 1965, but it would return for a seven-week season in 1970 and 1972, and reappear for a six-week run in 1974. Two ill-advised full-length movies were made, as well as a couple of more successful Christmas specials.

Its appeal not confined to Britain, *Steptoe and Son* would be bought for the US in 1970 by American producer Norman Lear and, with black actors Redd Foxx and Desmond Wilson, become a huge hit as *Sanford and Son.* Even the Dutch got into the act, with their version called *Siefbeen en Zoon.*

Cyprus Crisis Deepens

Never far from world headlines as its Greek and Turkish communities argued and fought over territory and civil rights, the Mediterranean island of Cyprus looked set to explode once more this month as Archbishop Makarios, the Greek community leader and President of Cyprus since independence in 1960, threatened to tear up all existing treaties between Greece, Turkey and Britain in a New Year's message on January 1.

Within days, the British Government issued invitations to all parties for talks in London. Any hopes of reconciliation or compromise were dashed, however, on January 28 when Turkish delegates led by Prime Minister Inonu stormed out of the meeting and returned home, demanding that the United Nations intervene to secure the rights of Turkish Cypriots.

Goldwater To Run For The White House

IN AN UNEXPECTED move today, Senator Barry Goldwater - who was best known as the standard bearer for extreme right wing, ultra-conservative political beliefs - announced that he would seek the Republican nomination for the US Presidential election due to take place at the end of the year.

The election would be crucial - did America want to persevere with the Democrats after John F Kennedy's assassination in November last year, or was the pace of reform and liberalization he'd initiated proving too fast for the majority of Americans?

Goldwater would undoubtedly attract considerable support from southern whites who, while traditionally Democratic Party stalwarts, had been clearly unhappy with Kennedy's support for the civil rights movement of Dr Martin Luther King, and were known to be disenchanted that President Johnson - a Texan - had vowed to continue with his dead predecessor's reform programme.

However, some of Goldwater's more extreme statements (he'd proposed a nuclear strike on North Vietnam to get the war over and US boys back home), were unlikely to appeal to the more enlightened Republican Party members in the American heartland.

It was going to be an interesting election year.

Black Producer For Folk Star Dylan

Fast-rising folk singer Bob Dylan's third LP was released in America this month. Titled *The Times They Are A-Changin'*, it had been recorded at the end of the previous year with the civil rights movement at its height, and included many notable protest songs which would become among his most famous compositions.

The album also marked the first occasion on which Dylan had been produced by someone other than John Hammond, the man who had 'discovered' him in 1961 when Dylan played harmonica on an album by Texan folk singer Carolyn Hester. The new man was Tom Wilson, a young black producer CBS recommended when Dylan's manager asked for a replacement.

Quant Slams Frumpy French Fashions

A major force in fashion design, Mary Quant (pictured) - who, with her husband, Alexander Plunket-Greene, had opened *Bazaar*, Britain's first and trendiest boutique in Chelsea during the late 1950s - dared to criticize Paris couturiers as 'out of date' and old-fashioned in an interview today.

Obviously a woman not afraid to make enemies among the old guard, Quant added fuel to the fire by saying that young females were tired of wearing essentially the same clothes as their mothers, her view of what the French fashion houses were still offering in this season's shows.

The idea of Quant's boutiques was to make and display designs which were both fun and reasonably priced. Her Ginger Group was now spreading the word by designing for the American JC Penny chain of stores, proving that the 30 year old really had stolen the baton from long-established, but unimaginative, older rivals in Paris and New York.

America Goes Wild For The Beatles

THE INEVITABLE HAPPENED today when American teenagers were finally given the chance to catch their first glimpse of The Beatles, the Liverpool beat group who were changing the face of popular music just as dramatically as Elvis Presley had when he first emerged on the international stage in 1956. They went crazy, with thousands packing New York's Kennedy Airport to greet Pan Am's flight 101 from London, while every pop radio station broadcast non-stop Beatles music to help whip up the frenzy.

The Beatles had been the most popular group in Britain and Europe during the previous year, with three massive chart-topping singles and their first album also a No 1 hit. Because Capitol Records - who were contractually entitled to release the group's records in the US - had initially declined to do so, smaller independent labels had licensed those British hits. The group's US success had been fragmented until Capitol, embarrassed that the biggest group in Europe were almost totally unknown in the US, finally got into the driving seat by releasing The Beatles' fifth single *I Want To Hold Your Hand*.

Capitol had arranged an appearance for The Beatles on the top-rated *Ed Sullivan Show,* concerts in Washington,

New York and Miami, along with a series of promotional events.

It was all a riotous success. The scenes at Kennedy Airport were just the beginning, with an estimated 73 million people watching their live TV début on February 9 when they performed *All My Loving, Till There Was You, She Loves You, I Saw Her Standing There* and *I Want To Hold Your Hand* - the latter already lodged at No 1 in the US singles charts. The Beatles had progressed from virtual unknowns to major celebrities overnight.

The British invasion of the US pop music scene had begun, and nothing would be the same again.

Cyprus Erupts Into New Civil War

Months of increased tension, argument and hostility exploded into violence in Cyprus today as fighting broke out on the Mediterranean island, leaving 20 Turkish residents and one Greek dead.

The worst of the clashes were in the southern coastal town of Limassol, where British troops tried in vain to restore order. Both sides seemed intent on causing as much damage as possible to their opponents, with Turkish militia establishing machine-gun nests on high buildings and Greek forces occupying central areas of the city.

The Cyprus situation had deteriorated dramatically since the Turkish Government's walk-out of London peace talks last month. Reinforcements in the shape of 1,500 British servicemen were sent from Britain following the bombing of the US Embassy, and Soviet leader Nikita Khrushchev almost inevitably protested at what he called 'occupation by Nato'. Things would not improve for some time.

Peter Sellers Marries Swedish Beauty Britt

British film star Peter Sellers hoped it would be a case of third time lucky today when the 39 year old married 21 year old Swedish beauty Britt Ekland in London. His new bride was said to be an actress, but was best known for her photogenic qualities rather than for her abilities as a convincing leading lady.

Sellers, who'd become a star via his appearances on the surreal BBC radio series *The Goons,* had moved into films in the early 1950s, establishing himself with excellent performances in such British comedy classics as *The Lady Killers, The Mouse That Roared,* *I'm Alright, Jack* and *Only Two Can Play* before being spotted by Hollywood.

His first major international success had come in 1963 with *The Pink Panther* - in which he played Inspector Clousseau, an accident-prone French detective destined to become a long-running cult hero - and Stanley Kubrick's dark satire *Dr Strangelove,* in which he'd played all the male leads except one in an acting *tour de force*.

Sellers was also a notorious womaniser, and his marriage to Britt Ekland was doomed to failure.

ARRIVALS
Born this month:
29: James Ogilvy, son of Princess Alexandra and Angus Ogilvy

DEPARTURES
Died this month:
6: Emilo Aguinaldo, Philippine revolutionary, independence fighter
25: Maurice Farman, French aviation pioneer

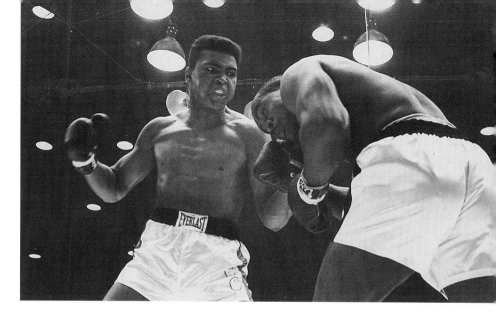

FEBRUARY 1

Belgian Nun Tops US Pop Charts

The hit parade constantly produces the unexpected but, before today, the US pop charts had never been topped by a nun from Belgium singing a song in French, apparently praising the advantages of the Dominican order to which she belonged.

The song was called *Dominique,* the artist was a 33 year old Belgian nun, Sister Luc-Gabrielle, who was billed simply as 'Soeur Sourire' (Sister Smile), and the song had been recorded in 1961 as one of a number intended to make a limited-release album to help her Brussels convent raise some funds. When executives at the Philips Records company heard the results, they'd decided to make it commercially available.

In late 1963, a US record label boss decided to release *Dominique* as a single, and an album titled *The Singing Nun.* With America still grieving President Kennedy's assassination, the gentle and melodic song was an instant success and topped the Billboard chart for four weeks. The album would spend 10 weeks at No 1, finally dislodged by the first US album by - The Beatles, of course!

Clay Defeats 'Unstoppable' Liston

AGAINST ALL ODDS - and the predictions of seasoned ring-watchers - the young and unfancied Cassius Clay defeated the fearsome Sonny Liston in Miami tonight to become the new world heavyweight boxing champion. Typically, his victory proved a controversial one when Liston simply threw in the towel.

Before the contest, Liston was hot favourite to retain his title, with bookmakers offering odds of 7-1 against ex-Olympic champion Clay, who was regarded by critics as a self-important loud-mouth. It was generally agreed that 31 year old Liston, an unpleasant thug with a devastating punch, would silence the brash 22 year old challenger, who was known as 'The Louisville Lip'. Clay had been dumped on the canvas by British heavyweight champion Henry Cooper in June 1963, but had recovered to defeat Cooper in the fifth round, as he'd predicted. If Cooper could catch Clay, the experts said, how could Clay survive against Liston?

At the weigh-in, Clay had justified his nickname with a continuous barrage of insults, but failed to provoke an impassive Liston into a response - although it did earn him a fine for bad behaviour. In the fight itself, Clay used his superior speed and fitness to keep Liston at bay for six rounds. Then, sensationally, the champion simply refused to come out for the seventh round, complaining of a serious shoulder injury. The self-confident underdog had defeated a Goliath. In the ensuing chaos, Clay was still talking too much, although he now had good reason to boast that he was The Greatest.

France And Britain Agree To Tunnel

After close on 100 years of thwarted plans, wacky ideas and inevitable distrust and rivalry, the governments of France and Britain finally agreed today to collaborate in the building of a tunnel to link the two countries.

The exercise, which was costed at £160 million ($300m), did not yet have a commencement date. That would have to wait until civil engineers and architects submitted their ideas and a design was selected.

In fact, it would be two more years before a target completion date of 1975 was set, but the project would founder that year (with nothing actually built anyway) when the Labour government pulled out. The Channel Tunnel would not be revived as a scheme until 1985, and would not actually open for business until 1994.

Moon Crash Sets Back US Space Programme

Locked into a tit-for-tat space race with the Soviet Union, and the determination of President Kennedy that a US astronaut would be first to set foot on the moon, the NASA bid to make that dream a reality suffered a set-back today when *Ranger 6* crashed on to the lunar surface without sending any images back from its cameras.

NASA's disappointment was all the greater following, as it did, their success on January 29, of launching a Sturn rocket with a 10-ton payload, the heaviest yet. The role of *Ranger 6* was to act as a vital reconnaissance device, sending close-up pictures of the moon to help US scientists establish the most ideal landing sites when NASA was able to send a manned craft.

Vigilante Ruby Appeals Against Electric Chair

IT CAME AS NO GREAT surprise today when a jury in Dallas, Texas, found Jack Ruby guilty of the murder of Lee Harvey Oswald, the man accused of assassinating President John F Kennedy. After all, millions had been watching Dallas police bringing Oswald through the garage of their headquarters when Ruby appeared out of a crowd of onlookers to shoot the supposed assassin dead.

With so many witnesses, Ruby could have had no hope of denying that he was guilty of the crime. But there was an element of sympathy for Ruby from those who considered that he'd merely avenged the President's killing. What they appeared to have forgotten was that Oswald had not been convicted of the killing in any trial, neither had he made any admission of guilt. Subsequently, there would always be considerable doubt about his involvement in the assassination.

Ruby, a nightclub owner with Mafia connections, was sentenced to death, after which his lawyers appeared on television to denounce the verdict as a 'violent' miscarriage of justice, announcing that they would lodge an appeal outside the jurisdiction of Dallas, where they believed their client would never receive a fair hearing.

Ruby would never face the electric chair. He died in prison on January 3, 1967, of a blood clot in his lung.

Taylor Goes For A Burton

The tempestuous on-off affair between Elizabeth Taylor and Richard Burton - begun in 1962 during filming of the epic *Cleopatra* in Rome under a very see-through veil of secrecy - reached a climax on the eighth floor of the Ritz-Carlton Hotel in Montreal today when they defied the cynics and tied the knot.

The couple's 'surprise' wedding (with carefully orchestrated 'exclusive' features and syndicated photo rights) was followed, according to the couple's spokesman, by 'a night of talk, laughter and tears'.

While the fiery Welsh actor did confirm that he was 'very, very happy', his bride did not comment. He had been married once before - and had been when they'd first met. Miss Taylor, however, had tied more knots than the average midshipman, having plighted her troth to the Hilton Hotel chain heir Nicky Hilton, English actor Michael Wilding, US film producer Mike Todd and former singing idol Eddie Fisher before Burton's Antony swept her Cleopatra off her feet.

A Third Son For Queen Elizabeth

The British Royal Family expanded once more today with the birth of a fourth child, and her third son, to Queen Elizabeth II and her husband, Prince Philip, the Duke Of Edinburgh.

The young prince, who was to be named Edward, followed the heir to the throne, Prince Charles (born November 14, 1948), Princess Anne (born August 15, 1950) and Prince Andrew (born February 19, 1960).

With the Queen approaching the age of 40, and a solid schedule of official duties until fairly late into her pregnancy, it was a concerned nation which learned, to its relief, that mother and son were both fit and well.

UN Sends Peace Force To Cyprus

As hostilities between warring Greek and Turkish factions accelerated in Cyprus, the United Nations today mobilized a peace-keeping force to separate the opposing communities.

Composed of troops from Britain, Canada, Ireland, Finland and Sweden, the UN force had been given a mandate to remain on the Mediterranean island for three months, an inappropriately brief time, according to some, although British Government sources were confident that would be enough.

Perhaps predictably, neither of the groups seemed prepared to co-operate with the UN, and promises were regularly broken. At one stage it resulted in British UN personnel being attacked after they'd brokered a ceasefire, while a planned evacuation of Turkish women and children had to be abandoned in the face of Greek intransigence.

Born this month:

10: HRH Prince Edward, UK theatrical and TV entrepreneur (see main story); Neneh Cherry, US pop/jazz singer (*Buffalo Stance, Manchild*, etc)

15: Rockwell (Kennedy Gordy), US singer, songwriter, (son of Berry Gordy Jr, founder of Motown Records)

17: Rob Lowe, US film actor (*St Elmo's Fire, Hotel New Hampshire, Youngblood*, etc)

19: Courtney Pine, UK jazz saxophonist, writer, arranger

26: Billy Warlock, US TV actor (*Happy Days, Young And Restless, Baywatch*)

30: Tracy Chapman, US folk singer, songwriter, Grammy Award winner (*Fast Car, Crossroads*, etc)

DEPARTURES

Died this month:

6: King Paul I, Greek sovereign

20: Brendan Behan, Irish playwright (*Borstal Boy, The Hostage, The Quare Fellow*, etc), aged 41

MARCH 30

Mods And Rockers Clash At Clacton

While popular history has the Sixties as the decade of peace, love and understanding, there were those determined to ensure there was still an ugly side to life. Two groups of them, Britain's Mods and Rockers, came together for the first time in the Essex coastal resort of Clacton today with the simple idea of beating each other up.

In shorthand terms, Mods were dedicated followers of fashion, loved The Who, motor scooters and amphetamines, while Rockers wore greasy leathers, rode motorbikes and clung to 1950s rock 'n' roll music. The two never should meet, and when they did there was bound to be trouble.

Arrests were made, noses and worse were bloodied, a peaceful seaside town was terrified. It would get worse as the summer progressed.

MARCH 28

Pirates Waive The Rules In Pop Revolution

It was a historic day for pop music in Britain and Europe as Radio Caroline began transmitting a new type of programme - 24-hours-a-day, non-stop rock - from a ship (pictured) moored just outside British territorial waters off the Essex coast. Within weeks, Caroline would be followed by others, all of them described as 'pirates' by a furious British Government and a concerned BBC. First on-air was a young disc-jockey called Simon Dee. By the summer he'd be joined by an equally youthful Tony Blackburn, both of them destined to become household names while Irish entrepreneur Ronan O'Rahilly, the man who'd spotted the legal loophole, started to make lots of money from advertisers keen to reach the pirates' avid listeners.

A Busy Month for the Beatles

It would be easy to fill all the March pages with Beatles stories - they were everywhere you looked! To give you a flavour of their lives since becoming the biggest thing since Elvis, here are a few news items from this month alone:

The group were named as Showbusiness Personalities of the Year at the Variety Club's annual dinner at London's Savoy Hotel....they became the first-ever pop stars to have their images displayed at the world-famous Madame Tussauds waxworks....Ringo Starr was elected Honorary Vice-President of Leeds University....John Lennon published his prose-and-poetry book *In His Own Write*, which would subsequently win the prestigious Foyle's Literary Prize....Paul McCartney made an appearance on the top TV show *Ready, Steady, Go* to deny that he and actress Jane Asher had secretly married....The Beatles began filming their first movie, *A Hard Day's Night*....All top six positions in the Australian charts were taken by Beatles singles - *I Saw Her Standing There, Love Me Do, Roll Over Beethoven, All My Loving, She Loves You* and *I Want To Hold Your Hand*....Official trade figures in the US revealed that 60 per cent of all records sold there in the past year were by The Beatles.

Great Train Robbers Found Guilty

AUGUST 8, 1963, was the day when a 20-strong gang carried out an audacious plan to rob a Royal Mail train in Buckinghamshire, escaping with over £2.6 million. Almost inevitably - with so many people and so much money involved - British police were soon on the trail of the culprits, and the net began to close on them.

Today, after a 51-day trial at Buckinghamshire Assizes, ten of those caught and accused of the Great Train Robbery were convicted of offences connected with the hold-up - the biggest yet in British criminal history. Nine others still awaited trial.

All in all, the Great Train Robbery established all kinds of records: for the size of the haul itself, for the length of the trial, the 66 hours it had taken the jury to reach their guilty verdicts - and for the sentences handed out.

Seven of the men - Gordon Goody, Bob Welch, Roy James, Tommy Wisbey, Jim Hussey, Charlie Wilson and Ronnie Biggs - were each jailed for 30 years, with Roger Cordrey given 14 years. There was public outrage. While many murderers were only given 15 years, the Great Train Robbers were, it was believed, being singled out for the wrath of the establishment.

At least one of the gang, the redoubtable Ronnie Biggs, would agree with that opinion and escape in July 1965, never to return to Britain again, despite the best efforts of Scotland Yard, British diplomats and a kidnap gang. But that's another story.

NO NOMINATION FOR MARNI AS 'MY FAIR LADY' STEALS OSCARS

Marni Nixon didn't get nominated for an Oscar this year, just as she didn't in 1961, when her unrecognized performance also played a key part in helping a hit film win the Best Picture prize in the Academy Awards.

Puzzled? OK, Marni Nixon was the singer whose voice was used for the soundtrack of *West Side Story* three years ago, and also featured to the fore in *My Fair Lady* this year. In the first case it helped a non-singing Natalie Wood portray Maria, and this year a similarly-handicapped Audrey Hepburn's Eliza Doolittle mimed to the Nixon recording.

Poetic justice of a sort was achieved in the fact that neither of the non-singing actresses were nominated for those particular films, though there seems little justice at all in the fact that Marni Nixon's contributions to film history have not even been recognized with an Honorary Oscar.

Ironically, the singing star who'd made the stage version of *My Fair Lady* a smash on Broadway and in London - Julie Andrews - and who'd been turned down for the movie, got sweet revenge by winning the Best Actress award for *Mary Poppins*. Thankfully, Dick Van Dyke's appalling cockney chimney-sweep didn't get him a mention anywhere.

In competition with Stanley Kubrick's *Dr Strangelove* or, *How I Learned to Stop Worrying and Love the Bomb* (longest-titled nominee in history), *Mary Poppins, Becket* and *Zorba the Greek,* the musical won the Best Picture prize, a Best Director Oscar for George Cukor, and a second Best Actor in succession for Rex Harrison, who'd picked up one for *Cleopatra* in 1963.

Peter Sellers should, by rights, have been nominated three times over for his roles in *Dr Strangelove,* and Richard Burton proved that he could still act the pants off almost anyone with his performance in *Becket* - especially when he was matched with the likes of Peter O'Toole, who was also nominated as Best Actor.

But the year belonged to *My Fair Lady.* It finished up with ten nominations and won nine Oscars. The only one to lose out was Stanley Holloway, who was pipped for the Supporting Actor award by Peter Ustinov. His prize, for the gem robbery thriller *Topkapi*, made a matching pair with the one he'd won in 1960, for *Spartacus.*

Audrey Hepburn and Rex Harrison in the Oscar winning My Fair Lady

APRIL 5

Last Post For General MacArthur

General Douglas MacArthur, one of the most remarkable military figures in modern history and a genuine superstar with the US public for close on 10 years as he broke rules, spoke his mind and drove his enemies back, died today at the age of 84.

MacArthur in fact enjoyed two careers. The first ended with his retirement in 1937, after he'd seen distinguished service in the Philippines (where he was also made a Field Marshal in the Filipino Army) and France (in 1918) before becoming Superintendent of his Alma Mater, the West Point Military Academy, and US Army Chief of Staff. In 1941, with the US suddenly part of World War II after the Japanese attack on Pearl Harbor, MacArthur was recalled to duty as commander of US forces in the Far East.

After suffering a rare defeat by the Japanese in the Philippines (when he famously vowed 'I shall return'), MacArthur became Supreme Allied Commander in the South-West Pacific and honoured his pledge in 1945 after a daring island-by-island campaign.

In 1950, after spending five years as Supreme Commander of the Allied occupation force in Japan, MacArthur took command of UN forces in Korea, driving the invading North Korean forces back. When he made public his view that the UN should carry on through North Korea and take on the Chinese communists, President Harry Truman fired him. This time, Douglas MacArthur would not return.

APRIL 18

Orton Entertains With Mr Sloane

A new star was born in London's theatreland tonight when *The Entertaining Mr Sloane,* the first play by Leicester-born newcomer Joe Orton, received its première performance at the Royal Court Theatre. The audience loved it, and leading critics were quick to lavish praise on what was a potent mixture of vulgarity and sophisticated wit. Orton, who was 33, was very much a man of the times. An unashamed and undisguised homosexual, he was determined to make his plays every bit as daring and outrageous as his own private life. He succeeded, not only with tonight's instant hit - which would be filmed in 1969 with Beryl Reid and Peter McEnery - but also with *Loot* and *What The Butler Saw.*

His career, and life, would be cut tragically short in 1967, when his live-in lover, the artist Kenneth Halliwell, beat him to death before committing suicide.

Spy Exchange: Lonsdale To Russia, Wynne To Britain

BRITISH BUSINESSMAN Greville Wynne (pictured) – imprisoned as a spy in the USSR after being arrested by the KGB while on a sales trip to Budapest in November, 1962 – was released today in exchange for Gordon Lonsdale, the Soviet agent jailed by Britain in 1961 as leader of the Portland spy ring.

Wynne was freed after serving less than 18 months of his eight year sentence, and in a scene which would inspire many a future spy movie cliff-hanger ending, was exchanged at a border crossing in Berlin for the Canadian who'd passed the Soviets data relating to the Royal Navy's sub-aqua warfare research department in Dorset, crimes for which he'd been sentenced to 25 years.

Although he had apparently lost 40 lbs in weight during his spell in a Moscow jail, Wynne was at least still alive, which was more than could be said for his Russian contact, Colonel Oleg Penkovsky, who had been executed.

Wynne was still protesting his innocence to waiting pressmen. He was a salesman for a mobile display company, he said, and nothing more. His arrest, trial and sentence had been a Soviet tit-for-tat exercise in response to the arrest and imprisonment of the British Admiralty clerk, William Vassall, a month earlier. Wynne would not change his story until the 1990s, shortly before his death.

ARRIVALS
Born this month:
5: Marius Lacatus,
Romanian international
football player
23: Simon Matthews,
UK pop musician (Jesus
Jones)
25: Andy Bell, UK pop
singer (Erasure) *(See
Came & Went pages)*
28: Lady Helen Windsor,
daughter of the Duke and
Duchess of Kent

DEPARTURES
Died this month:
5: General Douglas
MacArthur, US military
commander in WWII and
Korea, aged 84
(see main story)
24: Gerhard Domagk,
German bacteriologist,
creator of the first
antibiotics
26: Edwin John Pratt,
Canadian poet

APRIL 4

Beatles Take Over US Singles Chart

ALTHOUGH AMERICA HAD BEEN pretty slow to pick up on The Beatles, once the initial impact had been made, anything and everything recorded by the group sold in prodigious quantities, to the point where they monopolized the week's charts in *Billboard,* the leading US trade magazine, today with an unprecedented twelve singles in the Top 100, including the entire top five!

Because Capitol Records had declined to release the group's first four British hit singles in the US, they had appeared on various independent labels. *Please Please Me* and *From Me To You,* for instance, were both released on Vee-Jay, *She Loves You* was on Swan, while *Love Me Do* - their first UK release in 1962 - was not released as a single at the time of their US chart domination.

Can't Buy Me Love (on Capitol) was at No 1, *Twist & Shout* (on Tollie, a Vee-Jay subsidiary) was at No 2, *She Loves You* (on Swan) at No 3, *I Want To Hold Your Hand* (on Capitol) at No 4, and *Please Please Me* (on Vee-Jay) at No 5, with *I Saw Her Standing There* (Capitol) at 31 and *From Me To You* (Vee-Jay) at 41. *Do You Want To Know A Secret* (Vee-Jay) was at 46, *All My Loving* (Capitol) at 58, *You Can't Do That* (Capitol) at 65, *Roll Over Beethoven* (Capitol) at 68 and *Thank You Girl* (Vee-Jay) at 79.

Both *All My Loving* and *Roll Over Beethoven* had reached the US chart as imports from Capitol Records of Canada, such was the demand for the Fab Four, while their complete dominance of the US was shown by the fact that they also occupied the top two places in the *Billboard* album chart, with *Meet The Beatles* (Capitol) at No 1 and *Introducing The Beatles* (Vee-Jay) keeping it company at No 2.

APRIL 13

Smith Is Rhodesia's New Leader

The white population of Southern Rhodesia put itself on a collision course with Britain and most of the African continent today when it voted Ian Smith, the 40 year old leader of the Rhodesian Front Party, as its new Prime Minister.

Smith, the son of a butcher and a World War II *Spitfire* pilot with the Royal Air Force, was a man openly dedicated to preserving white supremacy in a nation bound for independence.

Like the people who'd elected him to succeed the moderate and conciliatory Winston Field, Smith was determined that London would not force them to relinquish power. The loss of white supremacy, they believed, was the slippery slope to losing 'civilized standards'. He made a commitment to break with Britain and declare Southern Rhodesia unilaterally independent if the UK Government insisted on the black majority having full voting rights.

APRIL 26

Stones Start Rolling

Still with a lot of ground to make up before they could really claim to rival The Beatles, The Rolling Stones (pictured) - their latest hit *Not Fade Away* dropping off the UK singles charts - joined The Fab Four as one of the main attractions at London's Wembley Arena today. The event was the annual *New Musical Express* Pollwinners' Concert, which also featured on-stage appearances by The Dave Clark Five, Billy J Kramer & The Dakotas, The Searchers, The Merseybeats, Gerry & The Pacemakers, Manfred Mann and long-time UK favourites Cliff Richard and The Shadows. Many of those acts were about to launch themselves across the Atlantic in what would be called The British Invasion.

A week later, the Stones' first album - imaginatively titled T*he Rolling Stones* - would be released in the UK with more than 100,000 advance orders, replace *With The Beatles* at the top of the album charts, and sell enough to make an appearance in the UK Top 30 singles chart! The Stones were rolling...

APRIL 20

Mandela Confesses

When black South African leader Nelson Mandela finally addressed a packed courtroom in Pretoria, where he and eight other leading lights of the outlawed African National Congress (ANC) faced charges of conspiring to overthrow the South African Government, he virtually sealed his own fate with his eloquence.

'I do not deny that I planned sabotage', he said. 'We had either to accept inferiority or fight against it by violence'.

Mandela was brought to court from prison where he was already serving time for other offences against the apartheid regime. During his enforced absence, South African security forces had entered his home and seized ANC documents, plans and - most damaging of all - Mandela's own diary, which contained notes on guerrilla warfare.

MAY 18

Holiday Weekend Wrecked By Mod v Rocker Riots

THE ON-GOING ENMITY between Britain's opposing youth cults of Mods and Rockers reached a frightening new pitch of ferocity today to mar the traditional Whitsun holiday weekend.

Pitched battles were fought on the southern English beaches of Bournemouth, Brighton, Margate, Southend and Clacton - and as far north as the ancient city of Durham - as thousands of youths surged into the hated opposition with knives, bottles and sticks to do serious damage on each other.

Amid the mayhem and violence, many hundreds were arrested, with one magistrate echoing the opinion of most respectable citizens by describing those who appeared before him in the dock as 'little sawdust Caesars'.

British Home Secretary Henry Brooke responded to public and media outrage by promising 'firm action'. 'The streets of Britain are no place for such outrageous behaviour', he said.

MAY 14

Aswan Project On Course, So Nile Goes Off Course

Soviet leader Nikita Khrushchev and Egypt's President Gamal Abdel Nasser (pictured) today pressed a button to divert the mighty River Nile into a newly-built canal and enable Russian and Egyptian engineers to start the next phase of the controversial Aswan High Dam project.

The controversy was over the fact that while the dam would give Egypt double the amount of hydro-electric power it needed to fuel its growing industries and increase the amount of arable land in Egypt by 30 per cent, it would also raise the level of the Nile by 200 ft in places, submerging unique temples and tombs.

An international fund had already been mounted to save Egypt's architectural and historical heritage. Moves were already being taken to dismantle the entire Abu Simbel temple complex, stone by massive stone, and re-erect it further up a mountain side!

MAY 29

Russia Admits Satellite Spies

Confirming what everyone had long suspected, Soviet supremo Nikita Khrushchev admitted today that space satellites launched by the USSR were not only collecting scientific data to help its scientists in the space race, but had also been placed in orbit to allow the Soviet Union to spy on the activities of other countries.

This news came as little surprise to Western intelligence experts who had been indulging in similar behaviour for several years. But it did allow alarmists, conspiracy theorists and reds-under-the-beds pundits to tell us they'd told us so.

UK TOP 10 SINGLES

1: Don't Throw Your Love Away
- The Searchers
2: My Boy Lollipop
- Millie
3: Juliet
- The Four Pennies
4: I Believe
- The Bachelors
5: A World Without Love
- Peter & Gordon
6: Don't Let The Sun Catch You Crying
- Gerry & The Pacemakers
7: I Love You Because
- Jim Reeves
8: It's Over
- Roy Orbison
9: A Little Loving
- The Fourmost
10: Walk On By
- Dionne Warwick

ARRIVALS

Born this month:
1: Lady Sarah Armstrong-Jones, daughter of HRH Princess Margaret and Lord Snowdon
5: Kevin Saunderson, US techno-funk record producer, songwriter (Inner City), remix master (Neneh Cherry, Paula Abdul, etc); Lorraine McIntosh, UK pop singer (Deacon Blue)
11: John Parrot, UK snooker player, former world champion
26: Lenny Kravitz, US singer, songwriter (*Let Love Rule, It Ain't Over Til It's Over, Stand By My Woman,* etc)

DEPARTURES

Died this month:
1: Spike Jones, US comedy bandleader, parodist
2: Lady Nancy Astor, American born UK politician and women's rights campaigner
8: Joe Maini, US jazz saxophonist

MAY 27

Heart Attack Claims Indian Prime Minister Nehru

JAWAHARLAL NEHRU, the man who had served as Prime Minister of India since the country achieved independence in 1947, to become the world's most populous democracy, died of a heart attack at his home in New Delhi, today. He was 74 years old.

Nehru's death robbed India of its first great statesman, and the man who had piloted the subcontinent through an exceptionally difficult transition from British colonial rule to self-government, would prove almost impossible to replace. Much influenced by Mahatma Gandhi, Nehru had – in common with many colonial leaders – spent more than 18 years in prison during India's long fight for independence.

Since then, and his dedication to a political and military neutrality, he had emerged as a valuable and valued mediator between the great powers during the early days of the Cold War. When news of his death was made public, people wept openly and thousands filed past his body to pay their last respects as he lay in state.

Nehru's funeral took place on the bank of the holy River Ganges, and was attended by the British Prime Minister, Sir Alec Douglas-Home, Labour's deputy leader George Brown, and by Lord Mountbatten, who had been the last Viceroy of India before independence.

MAY 9

American R&B Hero Makes UK Début

American R&B star Chuck Berry (pictured), whose influence had been acknowledged by both The Beatles and The Rolling Stones, played his first ever British concert in London's Finsbury Park Astoria tonight, only weeks after completing a three-year prison sentence for an offence involving an under-age girl.

Raised in St Louis, Berry had been encouraged by the great bluesman Muddy Waters, who recommended him to Chess Records of Chicago. He recorded a series of classic hits for them, including *Johnny B Goode, Roll Over Beethoven* (which The Beatles had included on their second album), *Rock And Roll Music* (which they would feature on their fourth LP) and many more.

The first single released by The Rolling Stones had been their version of a fairly obscure Berry song, *Come On,* but they also included other Berry compositions in their stage show, including *The Jaguar & The Thunderbird, Memphis Tennessee* and *Sweet Little Sixteen.*

Berry had achieved fame in Britain while the law didn't allow him to take advantage of it. He made up for it tonight with a show which won him a standing ovation from a sell-out crowd.

Pirate Radio Revolution Spreads

The British authorities - both the government and the General Post Office - could only watch and listen helplessly today as a second 'pirate' station, Radio Atlanta, began transmitting 24-hour pop music from a ship anchored off the English east coast.

Both Atlanta and Radio Caroline, which had started the radio revolution in March, were within the tenets of British law by being outside territorial waters. While Atlanta's arrival was greeted with delight by UK and European pop fans able to pick up its signal, their joy was not shared by the establishment, especially the BBC, whose audience figures plummeted.

On May 27, the pirate ranks were swelled even further by the arrival of Radio Sutch, a station based on a disused War Department sea-fort in the Thames estuary and fronted by the eccentric English rock singer, Screaming Lord Sutch. It was going to be a Canute of a job to turn the tide.

MAY

Press Baron Beaverbrook Dies

Lord Beaverbrook, the Canadian born son of a Scottish Presbyterian minister who became a self-made millionaire by the age of thirty, emigrated to England to become a Member of Parliament, founded a newspaper publishing empire and became one of Winston Churchill's closest and most trusted aides during World War II, died today of cancer at the age of 85.

Max Aitken was, by any definition, a dynamic character who made as many enemies as friends during his eventful and remarkably successful life. A fervent supporter of the British Empire, he had been knighted within six years of arriving in England and shortly after became Chancellor of the Duchy of Lancaster and Minister of Information in the government of David Lloyd George.

Developing his publishing empire around his flagship *The Daily Express*, Beaverbrook was invited to join Churchill's war cabinet in 1940, acting in the key roles of Minister of Aircraft Production, Minister of Supply and Lord Privy Seal, as well as heading the first high-level Anglo-American mission to Moscow in 1941.

A staunch opponent of the Labour government which swept to power, he had also vociferously opposed the granting of independence to India and Pakistan.

Shastri Succeeds Nehru

Following the death last month of India's revered Prime Minister, Jawaharlal Nehru, the search for a successor capable of filling the huge gap he left in the country's political life had been resolved by the appointment of Lal Bahadur Shastri, who was sworn in today in Delhi.

Now 59 years old, Shastri had entered politics as one of Mahatma Gandhi's supporters and was widely respected for beliefs which, in the past, had led him to be imprisoned more than once. He took over the premiership from Gulzarilal Nanda, who had become caretaker Prime Minister on Nehru's unexpected death.

Martin Luther King Jailed, Three Vanish

The always inflammatory situation in America's Deep South was ignited again today when civil rights leader Dr Martin Luther King was sentenced to a term in prison for his efforts to force a restaurant in Florida to accept the federal law and serve black customers.

Worse was to follow, however, on June 23 when Goodman, Chaney and Schwerner - three young civil rights workers - vanished after being arrested by police in Mississippi. In the furore which followed, President Johnson would call in 200 naval personnel to help search local swamps and rivers while national civil rights leaders demanded that the whole state be put under federal control.

The bodies of all three would eventually be found, with a number of local police officers found guilty of complicity in their deaths.

Keeler Returns To The Real World

CHRISTINE KEELER (pictured), the former high-class call-girl and nude showgirl at the heart of the Profumo scandal which rocked the British establishment in 1963, was released from prison today after serving six of the nine months she'd been awarded for perjury and conspiracy to pervert the course of justice.

Keeler's sentence followed the jailing of West Indian jazz singer Aloysius 'Lucky' Gordon, one of her lovers, for assaulting her. In her evidence she had denied that two other men were in her apartment when she was attacked. She had, in fact, hidden them in her bedroom to protect their identities, and the reason for their association with her.

The 22 year old's notoriety came from her affairs with John Profumo, then Secretary of State for War, and Eugene Ivanov, a Soviet naval attaché. Confronted by allegations of security risks, Profumo had lied to Parliament when he denied being Keeler's lover.

When his lie was exposed, Profumo resigned – as did Prime Minister Harold Macmillan, some months later when it became clear that his handling of the crisis had damaged the government's image. Dr Stephen Ward, the society osteopath who'd introduced Keeler to Profumo and Ivanov, and ran an informal call-girl agency for his rich and powerful friends, committed suicide when it became obvious that he was about to be found guilty of procuring girls for sex.

UK TOP 10 SINGLES

1: You're My World
- Cilla Black
2: It's Over
- Roy Orbison
3: Someone, Someone
- Brian Poole & The Tremeloes
4: No Particular Place To Go
- Chuck Berry
5: Here I Go Again
- The Hollies
6: My Guy
- Mary Wells
7: The Rise And Fall Of Flingel Blunt
- The Shadows
8: Constantly
- Cliff Richard
9: Juliet
- The Four Pennies
10: Shout
- Lulu & The Luvvers

JUNE 4

Chichester Beats Atlantic Record

Britain gained a new and unlikely hero today when the 62 year old Devon-born Francis Chichester set a new record time for crossing the Atlantic when he arrived in New York, having completed the journey in his yacht, *Gipsy Moth III*, in less than 30 days. This bold adventurer, yachtsman and former aviator had also successfully battled lung cancer during the past four years, taking on a series of physical challenges to prove his recovery. Two years later, in *Gipsy Moth IV*, he would make an epic solo circumnavigation of the world, sailing from Plymouth to Sydney in 107 days, and back to Plymouth - by way of the treacherous Cape Horn - in 119 days. Returning to a hero's welcome, he would be knighted by the Queen, who'd use the same sword that Queen Elizabeth I had used to ennoble another great British mariner, Sir Francis Drake.

JUNE 23

Pope Outlaws The Pill

The introduction of the contraceptive pill had improved the lives of many women all over the world, but its acceptance by a substantial number in the civilized world had been muted - for religious reasons. The Roman Catholic Church regarded birth control by any means other than abstinence as sinful, a view which received an unconditional official stamp of authority today when Pope Paul issued an outright condemnation of the pill in an encyclical letter read from the pulpit of every Catholic Church.

The Pope's stance was greeted with relief by devout Roman Catholics and disbelief from others who found it difficult to credit that he could be so dogmatic about something which was of provable benefit to the vast majority of non-Catholic women for whom the pill offered release from a life of repeated pregnancies and consequent ill-health.

JUNE 22

It's John, Paul, George And... Jimmy!

The Beatles flew out from London today, on the first leg of their first world tour, without drummer Ringo Starr. He'd collapsed from exhaustion at a photo session only a day or so earlier and had been rushed to hospital.

Virtually at the eleventh hour, session drummer Jimmy Nichol (pictured) was asked to fill in, and within 24 hours he was a Beatle, playing on stage in Copenhagen, Denmark! The Fab Three & Nichol would perform concerts in Denmark, Holland, Hong Kong and South Australia until a recovered Ringo was able to join them.

Nichol would return to Britain with a bonus of £500 ($1,000) and a gold watch inscribed: From The Beatles and Brian Epstein to Jimmy - with appreciation and gratitude.

Mandela Receives Life Sentence

TO NO-ONE'S GREAT SURPRISE, but to widespread international outrage, Nelson Mandela, Walter Sisulu and six other African National Congress leaders were today found guilty of treason against the white South African apartheid regime and sentenced to life imprisonment. Unlike many countries, South Africa did not operate a parole system, so life meant just that.

The 45 year old Mandela did not display any emotion when he heard the verdict, even though he knew he would serve his sentence on Robben Island, the maximum security prison off Cape Town in the waters of Table Bay. Conditions there were harsh and inhuman, and the ANC men would be forced to labour day after day, year after year, in a lime quarry, allowed only one censored letter a week and one visitor every six months.

Mandela had been a civil rights activist since World War II, and while his law degree might have been useful in previous showdowns with the South African authorities, his decision to embark on armed resistance to apartheid had put him beyond the law and way past the point of compromise - even if compromise were possible.

As a police launch carried Mandela, Sisulu and the others to Robben Island later today, no-one could have known that Nelson Mandela would not only gain his freedom 27 long years later, but that he would justly become the first President of an apartheid-free Republic of South Africa once more an accepted member of the international community.

SCHOLLANDER SUPREME AS US SWIMMERS SCOOP TOKYO GOLDS

While most of the world media focused, as ever, on the more glamorous and photogenic events taking place in Tokyo's new Olympic Stadium, America found itself a new hero in the shape of Don Schollander, one of their all-conquering men's swimming team which took no fewer than nine of the twelve gold medals available, established seven new world records, matched another, and managed to collect an Olympic medal of some sort in every final. Not to be outdone, the US women's team set four new world records *en route* to collecting seven of the ten golds on offer.

But it was Schollander, the 18 year old from North Carolina, who was the brightest star in the US firmament. The first swimmer ever to win four gold medals at one Olympic Games, he got them solo in the 100m and 400m events, and both relays.

The only world record he did not beat was the 100m, but in the 4 x 200m relay he contributed a 1:55.6 split - two seconds faster than any other competitor - to help the US team deliver a winning time of 7:52.1, the first to break the eight-minute barrier!

It was a remarkable achievement for the young man, who would go on to study at Yale and win a fifth gold

medal in the 1968 Mexico Olympics.

Out in the open, US athletes were doing their bit to make *The Star Spangled Banner* one of the most-played melodies on the stadium loudspeakers. As expected, Henry Carr and Mike Larrabee took the two sprint golds while Dallas Long took the shotput title. Al Oerter won the discus, Hayes Jones took the 110m hurdles prize and Rex Cawley beat Britain's John Cooper to pick up the 400m hurdles winner's medal.

Fans of the New Zealand ace Peter Snell were thrilled by his achievement in becoming only the second man in Olympic history to win both the 800m and 1500m races, while the four-minute margin of Ethiopia's Abebe Bikila's victory in the marathon was all the more remarkable for the fact that he ran it barefoot!

But the biggest surprise on the track was not merely the defeat of the Australian world champion and hot favourite, Ron Clarke, in the 10,000m race (he was, surprisingly, beaten into third place by Tunisia's Mohammed Gammoudi), but that it was won by a relative unknown who beat his own previous best time by an astonishing 50 seconds.

Billy Mills, a part Sioux Indian US marine, came from

*Ann Packer wins
the Olympic 800m final*

absolutely nowhere to not only take the only gold medal of his life, but beat the Olympic record in the process. Asked if he'd been concerned about Mills during the race, a still-stunned Australian shook his head and said, 'Worry about him? I'd never even heard of him!'

British hopes of gold lay, in the main, with middle-distance ace Ann Packer and long-jumper Lynn Davies, a South Wales schoolteacher. Both came through in style, with Packer easily holding off the challenge of France's Maryvonne Dupureur to win the 800m final, while Davies - clearly used to the rain which hit the stadium during his event leaped to 26ft 5.5in (8.07m) to ensure himself a riotous welcome in the hillsides when he went home again to Wales.

But the Games belonged to Don Schollander, the four-time winner and three-time record breaker.

JULY 2

Johnson Signs Civil Rights Act As Mississippi Smoulders

WITH THE SIGNING of the Civil Rights Act of 1964 in Washington today, President Lyndon Johnson finally fulfilled the promise made by his predecessor, the late President John F Kennedy, to outlaw racial discrimination in the United States. The passing of the act was, however, too late to save the lives of the three civil rights workers who had been arrested in Mississippi and had then disappeared.

It was the final straw for most of those involved in the struggle for racial equality when, on August 4, their bodies were at last discovered and an FBI investigation began. To compound the outrage, a number of police officers and officials were found to have been involved in their murders.

The new Act made discrimination illegal in most aspects of life, including hotels and boarding houses, public facilities - parks and libraries, for example - and employment, including union membership.

President Johnson, who shook hands with civil rights leader Dr Martin Luther King as he formalized the Act, had been forced to work hard to prevent its message being diluted. The President appeared on television, asking the nation's support 'to eliminate the last vestiges of injustice in America', and exhorting his audience, 'Let us close the springs of racial poison'.

Princess Attends Beatles Movie Première

Princess Margaret was greeted by the sight - and deafening sound - of 10,000 screaming teenagers when she attended the world première of *A Hard Day's Night,* the first feature film starring The Beatles, in London this evening. Directed by American Richard Lester, the film was - to the surprise of many - shot in black and white.

The 'plot' of *A Hard Day's Night,* which had been devised by Lester and the group in conjunction with Liverpool playwright Alun Owen, was based on a fictitious and often surreal day in the life of The Beatles. Its suitably odd title was said to have been inspired by a remark by drummer Ringo Starr.

Among the 'real' actors who helped The Beatles become movie stars were Victor Spinetti and Wilfred Bramble - the latter best-known as television's curmudgeonly Albert Steptoe, but on this occasion playing Paul McCartney's fictitious uncle.

The film, crammed with new songs, would be greeted enthusiastically by The Beatles' millions of fans, and fairly warmly by the critics. But what else could they say about a movie starring the biggest pop stars in the universe?

Four days later a crowd of 150,000 packed the centre of Liverpool to welcome The Beatles home for the local opening of *A Hard Day's Night.* It would prove that for the 300 fans who were injured in the crush.

UK TOP 10 SINGLES

1: House Of The Rising Sun
- The Animals
2: Hold Me
- PJ Proby
3: It's Over
- Roy Orbison
4: It's All Over Now
- The Rolling Stones
5: I Won't Forget You
- Jim Reeves
6: Someone, Someone
- Brian Poole & The Tremeloes
7: You're No Good
- The Swinging Blue Jeans
8: Ramona
- The Bachelors
9: A Hard Day's Night
- The Beatles
10: Hello, Dolly
- Louis Armstrong

Country Star Reeves Dies In Plane Crash

Country & Western singing star Jim Reeves died today, just three weeks before his 41st birthday, when the private plane which he was piloting crashed just outside Nashville, Tennessee. Probably best known for his international million-selling hit, *He'll Have To Go,* Reeves' death was keenly felt and marked in Britain, where his gently sentimental style had found as much favour as it had in the US. He would remain one of the biggest country stars of all time, his records continuing to become best-sellers everywhere in the world long after his death. *(See Came & Went pages)*

New York Racked By Race Riots

RACE RIOTS IN New York State over three consecutive nights forced State Governor Nelson Rockefeller to mobilize the National Guard today in a bid to quell violence which resulted in over 500 arrests.

There was almost certainly some connection with the continuing civil rights struggle in the American South, which probably explained the riot involving thousands in the predominantly black area of Harlem on July 17. But authorities were less sure about later disturbances which were centred on the suburban and relatively affluent district of Rochester, several hundred miles away from the Big Apple on the banks of Lake Ontario. With the smallest percentage of unemployed workers in the entire 'Empire State', Rochester was regarded as a model of successful racial integration.

However, the death of two blacks when a police helicopter crashed into a building was felt to have sparked a riot in which mobs used home-made weapons and bombs against police. After an outbreak of looting, during which 500 people were arrested, a city-wide curfew was imposed.

Goldwater Confirmed As Johnson's Opponent

The battle lines in the forthcoming US presidential election were drawn clearly for the first time today in San Francisco when the Republican Party's national convention nominated Senator Barry Goldwater (pictured) as its candidate with an overwhelming 883 votes to 214. Although Goldwater had announced his candidacy in January, many believed his extreme right-wing posturing on a number of key issues - not least the Vietnam War, which he believed the US should end with a nuclear strike - meant he stood little or no chance of winning the job of trying to oust President Johnson from the White House. Goldwater himself was unapologetic about his views. Accused of being an extremist, he said 'Extremism in the defence of liberty is no crime'.
A convention motion condemning the ultra-right John Birch Society brought by New York's Governor Rockefeller was shouted down by a chant of 'We want Barry!'

JULY 29

Family Planning Clinic For Unweds

Despite a war of words and predictions that its arrival spelled the end of decency and civilization as we knew it, the first Brook Advisory Clinic opened for business in London today, with the controversial mission of giving family planning and other sexually-related advice to all who needed it, even unmarried couples.

With Britain in the midst of a youth revolution which inevitably included far greater licence for people to 'do their own thing', defenders of the Brook Clinics believed that such freedom should be accompanied by education. Grumps thought that teenagers just shouldn't do it.

JULY 27

Churchill Leaves Parliament For Last Time

Sir Winston Churchill, now 89 years old and increasingly frail, made his last ever appearance in the House of Commons today, having confirmed his decision to step down as a Member of Parliament. In keeping with his wishes there were no speeches, and no public demonstration of the sadness his departure inspired. The House was not about to let his leaving go without tribute, however, and the next day it paid the old war-horse the signal honour of passing an all-party motion recording parliament's gratitude for a remarkable life of service to Westminster, the nation and the world.

JULY 6

Yesterday Nyasaland, Today Malawi

Nyasaland became the latest African country to become independent today after many years as a British colony. Like most other nations, it adopted a name which better reflected its traditions - in this case, Malawi.

In common with many other newly independent African states, independence only came to Malawi after a long struggle, and found itself being led by a man who had been imprisoned by the British in the past. The arrest and incarceration of Dr Hastings Banda in 1959 had provoked riots which had left more than 50 people dead. After a year behind bars, Dr Banda had returned to lead Nyasaland to self-determination, becoming the country's first Prime Minister in 1961. To prove there was no ill-feeling in his heart towards Britain - and especially to Scotland, where he'd been a student - the ceremony to celebrate Malawi's birth was marked by a pipe band playing the Celtic melody, *A Scottish Soldier.*

AUG

Heart Attack Claims Fleming, James Bond's Creator

IT HAD BEEN SUGGESTED that the fictional secret agent, James Bond, was based - at least in part - on the man who created the legendary Double-O Seven. However, unlike his internationally famous creation, Ian Fleming (pictured) was not immortal, as was proved when he succumbed to a fatal heart attack today at the age of 56.

The ultra-suave Fleming had been educated at Eton before moving on to university. He also worked as a naval intelligence officer, as well as spending time in Moscow as local correspondent for *Reuters*, the international news agency. Both jobs undoubtedly provided insider knowledge which Fleming was able to incorporate into his Bond sagas, which began in 1953 with *Casino Royale*.

His highly successful novels (said to have been President John F Kennedy's favourite bed-time reading) were to become even bigger triumphs when they were adapted as feature films, with the similarly suave Scotsman, Sean Connery, playing the British secret agent licensed to kill. Even after Fleming's untimely death, new James Bond movies - and even books, written in the same literary style - continued to thrill readers and audiences around the world.

Great Train Robbery Update

Following the trial in March of ten members of the Great Train Robbery gang, the crime and its perpetrators seemed to show no sign of vanishing from Britain's newspapers, radio bulletins and television screens.

After sentences totalling over 300 years imprisonment were passed on a dozen gang members in April, the next significant event had come in July, when two members of the gang had their 25 year sentences quashed on appeal.

The news in August was no less gripping, though somewhat less welcome to the authorities - Charlie Wilson, one of the gang's ringleaders, escaped from Birmingham's Winson Green Prison on August 12 and simply vanished from sight.

Unknown to the police, Wilson had in fact been flown to Mexico, where he would join up with two other gang members, Bruce Reynolds and Ronald 'Buster' Edwards. Like them, Wilson would tire of endless sun and *sangria*, but while they would return to Britain, arrest and prison, Wilson moved to Montreal, where he would live until the long arm of the law stretched out to grab him in 1968.

Rock Pioneer Johnny Burnette Drowns

A contemporary of Elvis Presley - they attended the same high school in Memphis - pioneer rock'n'roller Johnny Burnette died today when he drowned during a fishing trip in Clear Lake, California. He was 30 years old.

Like Presley, Burnette first made an impression as an all-out rock'n'roll singer, leading a trio as singer/guitarist which was completed by his brother Dorsey and lead guitarist Paul Burlison. Their first single, *You're Undecided,* had been released in 1953, a full year before Presley's recording début.

Unable to break through to stardom, the Burnette brothers established themselves as hit songwriters, notably for Ricky Nelson, before Johnny returned to recording as a singer, scoring well with gentler material like *Dreamin'* and *You're Sixteen.*

Cyprus Conflict Rumbles On

Despite the mobilizing of United Nations troops in Cyprus to attempt to restore calm and prevent the opposing Turkish and Greek factions from continuing their conflict, there had been little peace in the Mediterranean island for some time.

Today witnessed the fiercest action for some time, when an estimated 64 Turkish air force jets attacked Greek Cypriot forces moving in on Turkish Cypriot positions in the northern coastal town of Kokkina, one of their last strongholds. The open involvement of the Turkish military would prove crucial.

As President Johnson entered the debate by pleading for both sides to talk, the UN would finally be able to broker a ceasefire on August 10. Praised as a triumph of diplomacy, it actually owed more to Turkey's escalation of the war by sending in its jets.

UK TOP 10 SINGLES

1: A Hard Day's Night
- The Beatles
2: Do Wah Diddy Diddy
- Manfred Mann
3: Call Up The Groups
- The Barron Knights
4: It's All Over Now
- The Rolling Stones
5: I Won't Forget You
- Jim Reeves
6: Tobacco Road
- The Nashville Teens
7: I Just Don't Know What To Do With Myself
- Dusty Springfield
8: I Get Around
- The Beach Boys
9: On The Beach
- Cliff Richard
10: Have I The Right?
- The Honeycombs

AUGUST 25

Yesterday Northern Rhodesia, Tomorrow Zambia

Just as Nyasaland had celebrated its independence last month by renaming itself Malawi, the neighbouring central African state of Northern Rhodesia also adopted a new identity when it was granted independence today.

Zambia was the name chosen, and the state's first President - elected unopposed - was to be the 40 year old Kenneth Kaunda (pictured) who'd worked as a teacher before entering politics.

Much was made of a story about a confrontation Kaunda was claimed to have had with a lion, which backed away when he had stared it down. The new President, it was said, had adopted similar tactics in his negotiations over independence, refusing to be intimidated by the British bulldog!

AUGUST 7

Johnson To Step Up Vietnam Action

US PRESIDENT LYNDON JOHNSON seemed determined to bring the war in Vietnam to a successful conclusion by supporting South Vietnam in its attempts to repel the communist Vietcong guerrillas and North Vietnamese government forces.

Today he asked Congress for permission to escalate US involvement in the war, his trump card being the discovery that a torpedo boat which had recently attacked a US destroyer in the Gulf of Tonkin was of Russian origin. A revenge air attack from US aircraft carriers had put 25 more torpedo boats out of commission, and also destroyed other key targets in North Vietnam.

While he received an almost unanimous vote of approval in Congress, the President was aware that some in the Capitol had expressed fears about committing US troops to an 'unwanted' war.

But he was eloquent in defence of his decisions to order the retaliatory attack, and to step up US involvement as a whole. 'There is no threat to any peaceful power from the United States', he said. 'But there can be no peace by aggression and no immunity from reply...That is why we have answered aggression with action'.

They were strong words which left no doubt about the President's readiness to commit America's formidable war machine to the South Vietnamese cause. But many felt that Johnson might live to regret his decision.

AUGUST 18

South Africa Barred From Olympics

With international revulsion over the life sentences handed out to Nelson Mandela and other African National Congress (ANC) leaders in June still fresh in their minds, and a growing anti-apartheid lobby working hard to isolate the South African regime from the rest of the world, the International Olympic Committee (IOC) today announced that no South African athletes would be permitted to take part in future Olympic Games - and certainly not the Games due to take place this October in Tokyo.

Representatives of the ANC and other civil rights and anti-apartheid movements had been supported by a number of national governments in the build-up to the IOC's meeting in Switzerland. Most powerful of all had been the threat of a boycott of the Games by most black African states and the possibility of the Soviet Union also staying away if South Africa were represented.

AUGUST 20

Portable TVs Arrive In Britain

Something of a standard in the US for some time now, the portable TV made its first bow in Britain today as one of the star attractions in the country's high street electrical stores.

Previewed in London, it proved to have an 11-inch screen, a 20-inch circular aerial, weigh only 16 lbs and be capable of picking up all three UK channels. Its manufacturers had high hopes that many of the 13 million British homes already boasting televisions could be persuaded to end arguments over which station to watch by buying one of their new marvels.

Dave Clark – The Real Number Two

While many British groups laid claim to being 'second only to The Beatles in the States', the truth is that for all of 1964 and 1965, only one really had a hold on that honour - London's Dave Clark Five. Taking full advantage of the breakthrough created by the Fab Four, the Five barrelled into the US, toured like demons, never said 'no' to a TV appearance, played the teen magazine interview game like a dream, and just became....huge.

It was an unlikely success story in many ways, because while The Beatles' songs were pretty sophisticated and often unusual, The Dave Clark Five's output was pretty basic, four-to-the-bar stomping with fairly mundane lyrics delivered, not by the man whose name featured in the group's title, but by keyboards player Mike Smith. Dave Clark was the smash-bash drummer.

He was also, it must be said, a very smart businessman with an even smarter manager - international concert impresario Harold Davison - who negotiated Clark some very clever deals to ensure that they kept most of the huge profits those hits, tours and TV dates would create. While The Beatles, for instance, received only a small percentage of their immense record sales in royalties, Davison and Clark actually owned The Dave Clark Five's recordings and merely leased them to EMI!

The US hits in 1964 were *Glad All Over, Bits And Pieces, Do You Love Me, Can't You See That She's Mine* and *Because,* while 1965 would see the band score with *Anyway You Want It, Come Home, I Like It Like That, Catch Us If You Can* and *Over And Over.*

Then it was over, pretty much. Smart enough to know when to call it a day, Dave Clark invested his fortune in property in London and the US to make an even bigger fortune, bought the world rights to the classic sixties TV pop series *Ready, Steady, Go!* and only seemed to slip when, in the late 1980s, he sank a fortune into the ill-fated rock stage musical *Time.*

PJ LETS RIP TO TEAR UP THE CHARTS

Bucking trends was always something PJ Proby seemed to excel at - that and tearing up the rule book. Certainly, his arrival and immediate success in Britain was very much against the flow of traffic, as was his choice of recording material which, while everyone else was trying hard to be original, consisted in the main of revived standards your mother couldn't find objectionable!

Born James Marcus Smith in Texas, and briefly known as Jett Powers in Los Angeles, where he was an unsuccessful rock singer and sometime TV and movie actor, he came to the attention of TV producer Jack Good, who'd been asked to produce and direct a British special for The Beatles. He decided to add Proby to the bill. With his dark lean good looks, his ponytail hairstyle, very tight velvet trousers and his big, sub-operatic voice, Good thought he'd make an impression.

That he did, and PJ Proby soon had three Top 10 hits under his belt - the raucous *Hold Me* and the big ballad offerings *Together* and *Somewhere.* While there were rumours of wild parties and excessive drinking, he ended 1964 on a natural high.

That became an all-time low in 1965 when, early in a UK concert tour, those tight velvet trousers gave out under the strain of a Proby leap and his nether regions burst into view. When it happened again a few nights later, the theatre chain banned him, as did a major TV company.

Fights with his management, rows with neighbours who didn't like all-night parties in swanky Chelsea, and an increasing drink problem proved too much. And while he'd continued to score hits in 1965 – most notably his over-the-top version of the *West Side Story* weepie *Maria* – when Proby's work visa ended in early 1966, so did his British sojourn.

The Dave Clark Five

MARIANNE – THE GOOD GIRL GONE BAD

Marianne Faithfull's impact on the London rock scene this summer was huge. From out of nowhere, this staggeringly beautiful convent schoolgirl whose mother was a Hungarian countess and whose ancestors included Leopold Sacher-Masoch, (the Victorian erotic novelist whose *Venus In Furs* helped coin the term 'masochism') came to epitomize the ideal of young and beautiful, and the decadent tinge our elders and betters saw in this new permissive revolution.

It also helped that she was managed by Andrew Oldham, The Rolling Stones' manager (if they weren't decadent, who was?), had often been seen in their company, and had

been given her first single by them.

As Tears Go By would become a huge hit in August, and while Marianne would not have another hit in 1964, her fame grew simply because of who she was.

In 1965 she'd have three more Top 10 hits (*Come And Stay With Me, This Little Bird* and *Summer Nights*) before beginning to concentrate on acting and creating the sort of headlines other young convent girls would have shown to them as dire warnings of what happened to good girls who went bad.

State Of Emergency As Indonesia Invades Malaysia

SEPTEMBER 3

MALAYSIA'S PRIME MINISTER, Tengku Abdul Rahman, declared a national state of emergency today and asked for the United Nations to intervene after Indonesian paratroops were dropped over Labis in central Malaysia. The invasion followed two years of intermittent strife centred on Indonesia's disapproval of the creation of Malaysia, which it considered still to be virtually a British colony which had 'stolen' the previously Indonesia-governed states of Borneo and Brunei.

It was a difficult time in the region, with race riots in Singapore and the threat of communist infiltration in Labis.

Britain, Australia and New Zealand had agreed that there was a need to strengthen Malaysia's armed forces to insure against an invasion from Indonesia, but the Indonesian action came too quickly for this to be put into effect.

British Chancellor of the Exchequer Reginald Maudling had attended a lengthy cabinet meeting in Kuala Lumpur, the Malaysian capital, after which the announcement of planned reinforcements had been made. The meeting had stopped short of sanctioning sea and air attacks on Indonesian targets, but today's events suggest that caution could be a thing of the past.

Rhodesia's Smith Arrives For Talks

Ian Smith (pictured), the newly-elected Prime Minister of Southern Rhodesia, arrived in London today to begin talks on the terms for his country's independence from Britain.

Before the talks even began, the former Royal Air Force pilot confirmed that while he knew how to spell the word 'compromise', it had no place in his political dictionary. If Britain insisted on Southern Rhodesia's black majority being given full voting rights, the whites Ian Smith represented would break away from the Commonwealth and declare themselves independent unilaterally.

Home Calls British General Election

British Prime Minister, Sir Alec Douglas-Home, dissolved parliament today and announced that a general election would be held in October. This would perform the dual function, Sir Alec presumably thought, of clearing the air after the 1963 sex and spy scandals and the lingering controversy over his own appointment in October when Harold Macmillan resigned, while taking advantage of the comparatively new Labour leadership of Harold Wilson.

Following the death of Hugh Gaitskell - whom many regarded as a relatively honest politician - in January 1963, the uneasy alliance between the scheming Harold Wilson and the short-fused George Brown, combined with endless bickering between Labour's left and right wings over many key policy areas. Sir Alec seemed to be in a reasonable position to be elected as Prime Minister in his own right, rather than being gifted the job by the Conservative Party's so-called 'Magic Circle' which included ex-Prime Ministers Winston Churchill and Harold Macmillan.

UK TOP 10 SINGLES

1: Have I The Right?
- The Honeycombs
2: You Really Got Me
- The Kinks
3: I Won't Forget You
- Jim Reeves
4: I Wouldn't Trade You For The World
- The Bachelors
5: The Crying Game
- Dave Berry
6: I'm Into Something Good
- Herman's Hermits
7: Rag Doll
- The Four Seasons
8: Do Wah Diddy Diddy
- Manfred Mann
9: As Tears Go By
- Marianne Faithfull
10: A Hard Day's Night
- The Beatles

Forth Bridge Links Edinburgh With Dunfermline

The Firth of Forth, a stretch of sea estuary on the east coast of Scotland, had forever forced road traffic to take a lengthy and time-consuming detour of nearly 30 miles to reach a part of the country which could be seen with the naked eye about two miles across the water.

Today's official opening of the Forth road bridge - the longest of its type in Europe - put an end to such activities by connecting the drivers of Edinburgh, on the Firth's south bank, with Dunfermline on the north side, for the first time in history.

While the new bridge immediately became the subject of folklore about how long it took to paint, motorists were just delighted that they might never have to pass through such exotic but gridlocked hamlets as Skinflats or Newmills again - unless they chose to!

Eternal Silence For Harpo

FANS OF THE Marx Brothers, the comedy team whose hilarious movies made them international celebrities, were saddened today by the death of Harpo Marx at the age of 70. Harpo's trademark was that he never spoke on screen, communicating instead with a wide variety of exaggerated facial expressions, elaborate mime and often honking an old-fashioned motor horn to punctuate his zany antics.

There were originally five Marx Brothers in the family vaudeville troupe, but by the mid-1930s, both Gummo (real name Milton) and Zeppo (real name Herbert) had left the act, which thereafter consisted of Chico (real name Leonard, who died in 1961), Harpo (real name Adolph), and Groucho (real name Julius).

Harpo's nickname came from his expert playing of the harp, which became a feature of many Marx Brothers movies – Chico was also usually featured playing the piano in an expert, but eccentric style. Groucho played the fool.

Among the Marx Brothers' most successful movies were *Animal Crackers, A Night At The Opera, Duck Soup, A Day At The Races* and *A Night In Casablanca*. By 1950 – when all three were nearing their sixties – their appeal had faded, and they wisely decided to call it a day, although the dozen films they made between 1929 and 1946 remain timeless classics.

SEPTEMBER 3

Bobby To Run For Senate

Robert Kennedy, younger brother of the assassinated US President and now eldest son of one of America's most powerful political families, ended months of rumour today when he confirmed that he was stepping down as Attorney-General - the job he'd been given by JFK - and intended to run for the Senate in November's elections.

Although Bobby Kennedy had never run for public office before, he had proved himself a formidable figure and not merely his brother's gofer. He had masterminded JFK's 1960 election campaign and earlier, as chief counsel of the Senate Select Committee on Improper Activities in the Labour or Management Fields, had successfully investigated and prosecuted Jimmy Hoffa, the notorious Teamsters Union leader.

SEPTEMBER 27

Kennedy Assassination - Everyone's Fault, But No Conspiracy!

The Warren Commission report on the assassination of President John F Kennedy blamed several agencies - the Secret Service, the FBI and the Dallas police force - for serious mistakes in the security they had provided in Dallas on November 22 last year, but ruled out the possibility that the President had been the victim of a conspiracy.

The FBI's files on Oswald contained information which should have made him a prime candidate for extra surveillance during Kennedy's visit to Dallas, but they neglected to share this knowledge with the Secret Service, which was also singled out

for particular censure - for its underachievement and its shortage of staff.

According to the Commission, it had uncovered no evidence to suggest that either Lee Harvey Oswald or Jack Ruby (who had killed Oswald two days later) were anything but lone wolves acting on impulse.

The growing army of conspiracy theorists began to pick holes in the Warren Commission's findings, and the apparent gaps in the lists of witnesses interviewed. According to them, the Warren Report simply posed more questions than it answered.

Meg's A Midlands Motel Hit

Whatever it is about soap operas - and there seem to be as many theories to explain their popularity as there are sociologists - the British ATV company seemed to have a hit on its hands with a show it introduced quietly this year as an afternoon break for housewives.

Called *Crossroads*, it was based, like ATV itself, in a Midlands suburb

somewhere near Birmingham, where the flinty Meg Richardson ran the King's Oak Crossroads Motel. Meg was played by the veteran actress Noele Gordon, and the minor crises with which her life - and those of her family and staff - was beset had become something of a hit, with other stations in the independent television network

starting to pick it up.

Unbelievably, considering its shaky sets, leaky plots and often oaken acting, *Crossroads* was destined to run for 4,510 half-hour episodes before its doors were shut in 1988. Meg, perhaps wisely, had left the show in 1981, sailing off into the sunset aboard the QE2.

Labour Government For Britain After 13 Years

QUEEN ELIZABETH II had not even ascended to the throne, from which she had ruled for over ten years, when the last Labour government was elected in Britain, but the long gap since the days of Clement Attlee's premiership ended today when Harold Wilson (pictured) led his socialist colleagues to a narrow victory over Sir Alec Douglas-Home's Conservatives.

The final outcome gave Labour an overall majority of just four seats, the closest result for many years, in an election which many saw as a watershed comparable to the one in which Attlee assumed power at the end of World War II, when much of the current electorate was too young to vote.

For the first time, the parties were not led by men born during Queen Victoria's reign, and the electorate clearly preferred the modern approach of Wilson to the scandal and accident-prone party represented by the ex-Earl.

Britain had, by a whisker, elected a party which proposed public control of national assets, including water and steel. Wilson's first cabinet appointments included James Callaghan, Denis Healey, Barbara Castle, Richard Crossman and Roy Jenkins. With the unpredictable George Brown as his right hand man as First Secretary and Secretary of State for Economic Affairs, whatever else happened, British politics were not going to be dull.

UK TOP 10 SINGLES

1: Pretty Woman
- Roy Orbison
2: Where Did Our Love Go
- The Supremes
3: I'm Into Something Good
- Herman's Hermits
4: The Wedding
- Julie Rogers
5: Rag Doll
- The Four Seasons
6: When You Walk In The Room
- The Searchers
7: I Wouldn't Trade You For The World
- The Bachelors
8: I Won't Forget You
- Jim Reeves
9: (There's) Always Something There To Remind Me
- Sandie Shaw
10: I'm Crying
- The Animals

OCTOBER 25

Stones Fans Upset Sullivan

Several British beat groups had made successful American TV débuts on the all-powerful *Ed Sullivan Show*, including The Beatles and The Animals. The elderly and rather staid Sullivan had become perhaps the most influential host of a TV variety show, particularly after Elvis Presley's appearances in 1956.

Sullivan's risible onscreen interviews with rock'n'roll stars ('How old are you?', 'Where are you from, son?') may have been fine in the 1950s, but seemed patronizing in 1964, especially when the fans of the act concerned - Britain's bad-boys, The Rolling Stones - continued their deafening near-riot during the traditional chat. Sullivan was furious. 'I promise you they'll never be back on our show', he told the group's manager, Andrew Oldham. 'It took me 17 years to build this show, and I'm not going to have it destroyed in a matter of weeks!'

OCTOBER 16

Chinese Explode First Atom Bomb

The Republic of China exploded its first atomic bomb today, at a site close to the Russian border. The event was not unexpected - at least by the four countries which already possessed an atomic armoury, the US, the Soviet Union, Britain and France - but it was unwelcome.

Early Chinese research into atomic power had taken place with Soviet assistance, until philosophical differences tore that co-operation apart. The Chinese confirmation of the test was accompanied by a belligerent justification: nuclear defences for China had become necessary because of 'the ever-increasing nuclear threat' from the US.

OCTOBER 24

Martin Luther King Awarded Nobel Prize

American civil rights leader Dr Martin Luther King had his efforts to win equality for non-whites recognized and rewarded today by the Nobel Prize committee in Oslo, which awarded him the coveted Peace Prize, citing his use of non-violent protest as an example to all.

King's response to news of the honour was typically modest. He described it as 'a tribute to the discipline, wise restraint and majestic courage' of millions of sympathizers, both black and white.

In hospital for a check-up when told of his award, the 35 year old knew his struggle - which gained its first world headlines in 1956 when he masterminded a black boycott of bus services in Montgomery, Alabama, in protest against the segregation of seating - was not over.

Even if President Johnson's Civil Rights Act had made racial discrimination illegal, entrenched attitudes remained to be eliminated.

Khrushchev Kicked Out In Kremlin Coup

OVER SIX YEARS AFTER he assumed solo control of the USSR, 70 year old Nikita Khrushchev (pictured second left with Leonid Brezhnev on his left) was deposed today while he was on vacation at his country retreat on the Black Sea coast.

His Politburo colleagues accused Khrushchev of creating and enforcing poorly-conceived industrial and agricultural policies which had often damaged the party, the state and its citizens. The reality - as seen from the free world - was that the ex-pipe fitter had tempered the more extreme views of his recent predecessors, and had often made Russia seem more approachable to the non-communist world, even if his suppression of the 1956 Hungarian uprising proved he was quite prepared to use traditional bully-boy tactics to maintain the *status quo.*

There was also little doubt, according to seasoned Kremlin watchers, that Khrushchev's embarrassing defeat in the 1962 Cuban missile crisis stand-off against President Kennedy had been the moment when his departure became inevitable. That, and his occasional public slips in decorum, made him a liability.

On the positive side, Khrushchev had served his people well by debunking the personality cult surrounding his old boss, the tyrant Josef Stalin, moderating the powers of the secret police and dismantling most of the labour camps for political dissidents.

Khrushchev's successor as Communist Party leader was to be Leonid Brezhnev, while his role as Prime Minister went to Alexei Kosygin. Khrushchev himself would wander off into the obscurity of retirement, and die - his passing unmourned and unmarked by the current regime - in 1971.

Song Genius Cole Porter Signs Off

The death today of Cole Porter, regarded by many as the greatest songwriter of the century, robbed the world of one its wittiest lyricists and most melodic tunesmiths - the combination produced dozens of songs which remain popular classics.

Born in 1891, Porter came from a wealthy Indiana family and spent much of the 1920s living in Paris after serving in the French Army in World War I. A homosexual, Porter disguised his true nature with a celebrated marriage to socialite Linda Lee Thomas.

After returning to New York at the start of the 1930s, he produced an endless succession of standards, including *Night & Day, I Get A Kick Out Of You, Anything Goes, Let's Do It* and *In The Still Of The Night,* as well as hit revues and musicals such as *Kiss Me Kate* and *Rosalie.*

Herbert Hoover, Europe's Saviour, Dies

In many ways the epitome of The American Dream, Herbert Hoover - the 90 year old former US President who died today - was owed as much a debt of gratitude by the people of Europe as he was by his fellow Americans, who dumped him after only one term when his stay in the White House coincided with the Wall Street Crash of 1929. Born to a Quaker family in Iowa, Hoover studied geology and engineering before becoming

a mining engineer in Australia, China and Nevada and creating a private fortune. During World War I he gained world renown as head of the US' Relief Commission, organizing millions of tons of food and other supplies to Belgium, central Europe and Russia - powers which were extended at the end of the war to include the post of US Food Administrator and more aid for a desperate Europe.

Secretary of Commerce under Presidents Harding and Coolidge, in 1928 he won the Republican nomination for the Presidency, beating the Democrats' Al Smith to become the 31st incumbent of the White House. Within months of his election, the Wall Street Crash made his a lame duck presidency, and his defeat by Franklin Roosevelt in 1932 was a foregone conclusion.

ANDY BELL: GOT IT? FLAUNT IT!

As the voice of Erasure, the hugely successful British pop duo masterminded by synthesizer wizard, composer and songwriter Vince Clarke, the flamboyant Andy Bell - who was born today in Peterborough, Lincolnshire - has emerged as one of Europe's most popular singers, as well as becoming one of the gay movement's most articulate spokesmen.

Interestingly, his sexual orientation has done nothing to diminish the open affection in which the group's countless thousands of young female fans obviously hold Erasure. Certainly, they seem to love the increasingly outrageous outfits he selects for the duo's sell-out tours, most of which require a redefinition of (good-humoured) bad taste!

Musically trained as a choirboy, Andy had been a member of a local group before - along with 42 others - answering an audition advertisement in the UK pop paper *Melody Maker* in 1985 and being selected by Vince Clarke to join him in Erasure.

After a couple of so-so British chart appearances in early 1986, the greater European success of their fourth single, *Sometimes,* would finally result in a UK No 2 peak in December that year, after which Erasure have been able to do little wrong.

Huge hit singles since then have included *Victim Of Love, Ship Of Fools, Chains Of Love, A Little Respect, Drama!, Chorus, Love To Hate You* and their No 1 *Abba-Esque* EP, which was their tribute to the 1970s Swedish supergroup. In 1990, Andy and Vince were

Andy Bell

asked to step up at the annual Ivor Novello Awards lunch in London to accept a trophy recognizing that their *Blue Savannah* single was the year's most performed work.

Additionally, their international hit albums have included *Two Ring Circus*, *The Innocents* and *Wild!*, the last two of which entered the UK album charts at No 1. If and when Erasure decide to call it a day, few have any doubts that Andy Bell would be more than able to maintain his outstanding popularity.

JULY 31
JIM REEVES: GONE BUT NEVER FORGOTTEN

One of the most outstandingly successful country and pop performers of all time, Jim (James Travis) Reeves was, when the light plane he was piloting crashed in heavy woodland near Nashville today, destined to remain a best-selling artist for decades, his easy, relaxed style not dating as more distinctively-styled singers inevitably would.

Texas-born Reeves had aspirations to a professional baseball career until an ankle injury forced him into becoming an entertainer. That had always been a viable option for the singing guitarist - he made his radio début in 1935, at the age of 12.

Reeves' recording career began in 1950, but it was when he signed to RCA Records in 1955 and joined the regular cast of the influential Grand Ole Opry radio show that a string of huge international pop hits began - including *I Love You Because*, *He'll Have To Go*, *Welcome To My World*, *You're The Only Good Thing* and *Adios Amigo*.

The hits would continue for some time after his death because at least 80 unreleased tracks had been completed before the crash, so enabling RCA and his estate management to keep a flow of 'new' material coming to meet continued demand. Reeves also starred in a feature film, *Kimberley Jim*, which was made in South Africa, where he was especially popular.

MARCH 20
BRENDAN BEHAN: THE REALLY QUARE FELLOW

Brendan Behan's death today at the age of only 41 was remarkable to many, largely because the Dublin-born author and playwright had worked so assiduously for so long at killing himself with a hell-raising lifestyle. Which only begged the question: how much more could he have achieved if he hadn't spent so much time drunk?

A ferocious Irish nationalist, Behan found himself behind bars of a more sinister kind for the first time in 1939 when he was convicted of membership of the IRA.

Drawing on that experience - and others which brought him up against both the British and Irish authorities on numerous occasions - Behan would deal with all aspects of the Anglo-Irish conflict, tragic and humorous, in a series of powerful and often witty books and plays, including *Borstal Boy*, *The Hostage* and *The Quare Fellow*.

Ironically, it would be the London productions of the last two which would establish his formidable reputation, and it would be the arts establishment of the dreaded enemy, the English, which would be the first to recognize and lionize his talent.

Johnson Wipes Floor With Goldwater

ANY FEARS THAT THE extreme right-wing policies of Senator Barry Goldwater, the Republican challenger for the American presidency, would be popular enough to defeat the sitting President, Democrat Lyndon Johnson (pictured), were swept away today as Johnson won a landslide victory.

Johnson polled over 60 per cent of the popular vote, effectively ensuring a mandate to continue with the innovative reforms started by the assassinated President Kennedy, particularly in the elimination of segregation and poverty, although his Vice-Presidential running mate, Senator Hubert Humphrey, was at pains to emphasize that 'it was a mandate for unity, for a government that serves no special interest'.

The Johnson victory was seen as a triumph for moderation over extremism - some felt that the progress achieved in racial equality would be instantly lost if Goldwater were elected. The President had exhorted the electorate to join him in moving towards 'the Great Society where no child will go unfed, every human being has dignity and every worker has a job'.

The election also saw the two younger brothers of the martyred President Kennedy winning seats in the Senate. Edward Kennedy was re-elected in the Kennedy home state of Massachusetts, while Robert Kennedy, who, as Attorney-General in his brother John's team, had strongly pursued and enforced anti-racist policies, won in New York at his first attempt.

NOVEMBER 6

Brezhnev Tries To Heal Chinese Rift

Leonid Brezhnev, the new Soviet Communist Party chairman, today signalled his wish to reconcile the differences which had come to divide the USSR and the Chinese regime of Mao Tse-tung when he held talks in the Kremlin with a group of senior Beijing officials.

There were many advantages to both in negotiating a truce in the war of words which Mao and the deposed Nikita Khrushchev had started. Both nations were known to have positioned forces on their mutual border, mistrustful of the other's territorial ambitions, while the escalating conflict in Vietnam was one where both knew they should unite to help the North Vietnamese win.

Brits Still On A US Roll

Still spearheaded by the do-no-wrong Beatles, the British invasion of the US pop music scene was maintaining its momentum, with The Rolling Stones starting to show through - along with The Dave Clark Five - as main challengers to John, Paul, George and Ringo's crown.

This month, the US Top 20 chart summary showed The Honeycombs (with *Have I The Right?*), The Zombies (*She's Not There*), Manfred Mann (with their last-month No 1 *Do Wah Diddy Diddy*), The Kinks (*You Really Got Me*) and The Stones (*Time On My Side*) waving the Union Jack.

Interestingly, The Rolling Stones' hit, which would become the US No 1 early in December, would not be released as a single in Britain, while their UK No 1 - *Little Red Rooster* - would never be released as a single in the United States!

NOVEMBER 6

White Rhodesians Support Smith

Less than two weeks after Southern Rhodesian Prime Minister Ian Smith had been warned by the new British Prime Minister, Harold Wilson, that a unilateral declaration of independence (UDI) from British rule would amount to treason, a referendum almost unanimously came out in support of Smith.

Unlike many other African nations which had achieved independence only after demonstrating that progress was being made towards equality and democracy, neither Southern Rhodesia nor South Africa had any intention of reforming their white supremacist philosophies.

Southern Rhodesia was poised to join its southern neighbour as an international outcast with its minority regime subject to an increasingly vicious and bitter civil war, as its black majority fought to gain what was rightfully theirs.

UK TOP 10 SINGLES

1: Baby Love
- The Supremes
2: Pretty Woman
- Roy Orbison
3: Sha La La
- Manfred Mann
4: He's In Town
- The Rockin' Berries
5: All Day And All Of The Night
- The Kinks
6: Walk Away
- Matt Monro
7: Um Um Um Um Um Um
- Wayne Fontana & The Mindbenders
8: The Wedding
- Julie Rogers
9: When You Walk In The Room
- The Searchers
10: Tokyo Melody
- Helmut Zacharias Orchestra

Jinx Hits Martian Probes

Mars was the intended target for the latest space missions, as both the US and the Soviet Union aimed spacecraft at the so-called 'red planet'. However, both *Mariner 4* (launched by NASA from Cape Kennedy) and *Zond 2* (from the USSR) were today said to be experiencing problems which considerably limited the likelihood of much worthwhile information coming from these probes into the unknown.

Zond 2 was reported to be limping through the cosmos with only half its engines functioning properly, while the course plotted for *Mariner 4* - which was supposed to proceed via Canopus - had instead directed it to a smaller star in the same approximate vicinity.

This would result in it missing Mars by a considerable margin, but NASA technicians hoped to be able to partially correct the error so that the space vehicle would pass a mere 10,000 miles from its intended destination!

London - Wild scenes greeted a joint concert at the London Palladium by Judy Garland and her daughter, Liza Minnelli

Belgium Back In War-Torn Congo

LESS THAN FIVE YEARS AFTER being granted independence from its status as a Belgian colony, and only four months after Moise Tshombe had been sworn in as President, the West African country of Congo was again in turmoil, with Belgian paratroopers racing to the rescue of threatened white hostages today.

Another self-styled 'President' - a follower of the murdered Patrice Lumumba - named Christophe Gbenye had taken more than one thousand whites captive and was threatening to grill them alive. Quite what he meant by that was never established because Belgian troops descended on the rebel headquarters at Stanleyville, arriving just as Gbenye's soldiers began firing at the hostages in the city centre. Unfortunately, they arrived too late to save the lives of thirty whites, including three North Americans (two of them missionaries) and two Belgian children. The paratroops had been requested by the Congolese Government, but their rescue mission was called 'a criminal act' by the Soviet Union, which had been supporting the rebels.

Pope Sells 'Family Jewels'

Critics of the Roman Catholic Church, who had long cited the many riches of the Vatican as an incongruous and ostentatious display of unnecessary wealth while millions of the Church's followers lived in abject poverty, had some of the ground cut away from beneath their feet today. Pope Paul VI announced that he was putting one of his most valuable assets - a jewelled tiara estimated to be worth many millions in auction - up for sale. The proceeds were to be used to establish a new poverty relief fund.

Fresh Assault On Vietcong By Saigon

The South Vietnamese armed forces, strongly supported by American air power, descended on a forest near Thudaumot, some 40 miles outside Saigon, to fight with communist Vietcong guerrillas today, only to find that the enemy had fled the area.

Despite the assertions of the new Vietnamese leader, Tran Van Huong, that the Vietcong would be actively pursued - as the assistance of more than 100 US helicopters in airlifting thousands of Vietnamese soldiers attested - it was starting to look as if sympathizers had tipped off the Vietcong, which added another problem for the anti-communist alliance.

Still more Americans would soon be drafted to fight for a cause which they didn't necessarily support, in an alien South-East Asian country to which they owed no personal allegiance. The Vietnam War was beginning to change America's view of itself and its international responsibilities, and not everyone agreed that US troops should be sent to die for a questionable regime which would declare a state of martial law only seven days later as student riots paralyzed Saigon.

Kenyatta Is New Kenyan Republic's First President

JOMO KENYATTA (pictured with the The Duke of Edinburgh) became President of the new African republic of Kenya today, just one year after he'd steered his country to initial independence from Britain as its first Prime Minister. Kenya was to remain a member of the British Commonwealth.

Two weeks before he was installed as President and Kenya changed its status, the 50 year old Kenyatta had ruled that it would become a one-party state, effectively outlawing all political opposition to his complete authority. This would have provoked even greater concern had not the British High Commissioner, Malcolm MacDonald, described Kenyatta as 'the wisest bird in the whole of Africa'.

This compliment almost certainly resulted from Kenyatta's invitation to Inspector Ian Henderson, the white policeman who had arrested him on terrorist charges during the struggle for independence in the 1950s, to remain in his post, so allaying the fears of Kenya's white and Asian population that the newly independent state would become the venue for a vengeful bloodbath.

Baptized Johnstone Kamau, Kenyatta had lived in England, where he married an Englishwoman and wrote a definitive history of his Kikuyu tribe's customs. Returning to Kenya to help the fight for independence, he'd adopted the name Jomo 'Burning Spear' Kenyatta, and become the nation's most wanted man when the Mau Mau movement - a secret society formed by Kikuyu tribesmen - began a murderous guerrilla campaign against the British and non-compliant black Kenyans.

Death Of Marks & Sparks Chairman

Lord Marks, the man who built his father's string of cut-price 'penny bazaar' shops into the world-renowned Marks and Spencer chain of high street stores, died today at the age of 76. 'Marks and Sparks', as it was familiarly known to millions of British shoppers, had won a well-deserved reputation as the favourite clothing shop for those who demanded high quality without exorbitant cost.

Simon Marks had joined the infant company in 1907, served in World War I and returned to become chairman in 1916. With his life-long friend and partner Israel Sieff he transformed Marks and Spencer into an international leader.

Lord Marks had once said that his aim was 'to glamorize women and children at a price they can afford', and by the end of this century, several generations can attest to his success. Much of his personal wealth was donated to medical research and the Zionist movement, a commitment which had made his name a regular entry on terrorist hit lists.

Beach Boy Brian Breaks Down

There was to be precious little *Fun Fun Fun* for Brian Wilson, the oldest of the three Wilson brothers who were the nucleus of Californian hit group The Beach Boys, who suffered a nervous breakdown today during a flight to Texas at the start of the group's latest two week tour, and was rushed to hospital.

Wilson - The Beach Boys' main songwriter, producer, arranger and musician, as well as harmony vocalist - was known to be under considerable pressure from both Capitol Records and his immensely ambitious father, who'd been the group's manager until Wilson sacked him earlier in the year.

The group had enjoyed immense success in a very short time, having released seven albums in two years, all but one of which had reached the Top 10 of the US charts, as well as scoring sixteen hit singles in the same time.

UK TOP 10 SINGLES

1: I Feel Fine
- The Beatles
2: I'm Gonna Be Strong
- Gene Pitney
3: Downtown
- Petula Clark
4: Little Red Rooster
- The Rolling Stones
5: Walk Tall
- Val Doonican
6: Pretty Woman
- Roy Orbison
7: Baby Love
- The Supremes
8: I Understand
- Freddie & The Dreamers
9: There's A Heartache Following Me
- Jim Reeves
10: All Day And All Of The Night
- The Kinks

DECEMBER 21

Britain Votes To Abolish Death Penalty

THERE HAD BEEN GROWING controversy over Britain's continued use of the death penalty – which many saw as barbaric and unnecessary – as the ultimate punishment. And while its opponents welcomed today's House of Commons vote to abolish the gallows, no-one believed the arguments were over.

Two thirds of the votes cast by Members of Parliament favoured the end of the death penalty, although the decision was by no means a comfortable walk-over.

While there was no question of the House Of Lords (which had still to ratify the new legislation) overturning the decision, there were situations in which many felt the death penalty should remain applicable – such as killing for a second time, or the murder of a police officer. The immediate effect of the vote, however, was that convicted murderers awaiting the death penalty would instead serve life sentences – an early Christmas present for them all!

The debate would – and still does – continue to rage, and it would, in fact, not be until 1969 that the final nail was driven into the subject. Today's vote merely suspended (excuse the pun!) hanging for a trial period, although no-one was hanged between today and December 18, 1969, when the House of Lords finally voted for full abolition.

Soul Star Sam Cooke Shot

Sam Cooke, one of America's best-loved and most successful soul and pop singers, was shot dead at a motel in Los Angeles this evening, six weeks short of his 34th birthday. Police were said to be questioning the female manager of the Hacienda Motel, who claimed that Cooke had been trying to rape a 22 year old woman, and had also tried to rape her, the hotel manager - in his anger at being interrupted.

Like many black soul stars, Cooke - the son of a Baptist minister - was first attracted to music played in church, and his first recordings were made as a member of the gospel group, The Soul Stirrers. After he recorded secular material he was forced to leave the group, but scored an almost immediate US No 1 hit with *You Send Me* in late 1957.

Regular hits followed, with *Chain Gang* (1960), *Twistin' The Night Away* (1962) and *Another Saturday Night* (1963) all reaching the US Top 10. Many of his other hits - most of them self-composed - were recorded by British artists, among them Craig Douglas with *Only Sixteen*, Herman's Hermits with *Wonderful World*, and The Animals with *Bring It On Home To Me*.

End Of The Line For Beeching

One of Britain's favourite 'villains', British Railways chief Dr Richard Beeching, was unceremoniously fired by the new Labour government today, only 18 months after publishing his report *The Reshaping of British Railways* - a bombshell which recommended closing down 2,128 stations, axing almost 68,000 jobs and cutting the UK rail network in many remote rural areas.

The subject of vilification and attack by the rail unions and the Opposition, Dr Beeching, who'd been a senior director of the chemical giant ICI before the Conservatives invited him to head British Railways, must have known his days were numbered once Labour came to power.

His recommendations were not entirely ignored, however. In February 1965 the new British Railways board would announce it intended to slash the network by half, following guidelines established in Beeching's report.

Beatles – A Year-End Report

Just time and space for a recap on the fantastic year experienced by The Beatles as they swept to an unprecedented and unqualified domination of the world of popular music. Apart from causing riots wherever they played, they'd smashed every sales record imaginable, including box-office receipts for their first film *A Hard Day's Night*. John Lennon and Paul McCartney had leapt into the record books as songwriters - not merely for the numbers recorded, released and huge hits for The Beatles, but also for the innumerable hits scored by others with their songs. More than anywhere else, they had stormed and conquered Fortress USA, scoring no less than 30 hit singles, including six chart-toppers. Ending the year as they obviously intended to start 1965, their newest single, *I Feel Fine*, was No 1 in Britain and the US.

YOUR 1964 HOROSCOPE

Unlike most Western horoscope systems which group astrological signs into month-long periods based on the influence of 12 constellations, the Chinese believe that those born in the same year of their calendar share common qualities, traits and weaknesses with one of 12 animals - Rat, Ox, Tiger, Rabbit, Dragon, Snake, Horse, Sheep, Monkey, Rooster, Dog or Pig.

They also allocate the general attributes of five natural elements - Earth, Fire, Metal, Water, Wood - and an overall positive or negative aspect to each sign to summarize its qualities.

If you were born between January 25, 1963 and February 12, 1964, you are a Rabbit. As this book is devoted to the events of 1964, let's take a look at the sign which governs those born between February 13 that year and February 1, 1965 - The Year of The Dragon.

THE DRAGON
FEBRUARY 13, 1964 - FEBRUARY 1, 1965
ELEMENT: WATER   ASPECT: +

Dragons are mysterious, exotic people who exude sexuality. They are libidinous and very popular with the opposite sex. Adaptable and accommodating, Dragons fit in with whatever is going on around them. But they are also self-determined and won't submit to being dominated by others, so despite appearing agreeable and adaptable, they can be ferocious and dangerous.

Dragons are essentially powerful people, being kind and generous when allowed to take the lead. They are often found in positions of authority because they prefer to be in charge. It's no coincidence the Dragon is the symbol of the power and magnificence of the Chinese emperor.

Intellectually, Dragons are clever, bright and sharp, though they will throw all logic aside to follow their intuition. Things invariably work out well on these occasions because Dragons also tend to be lucky and land on their feet.

The Dragon is the luckiest of all signs and good fortune follows wherever they go. They also have the Midas touch, so the Year of the Dragon is good for business and money-making schemes. Dragons attract money and generally enjoy financial prosperity. Because of their easy-come attitude to money, Dragons are generous and hardly ever broke.

Dragons are also gifted creatures with an original turn of mind. They can be ingenious and resourceful, picking themselves up when they're down, whether physically, psychologically or materially to make fabulous come-backs. They never say die, never accept defeat and can be guaranteed to live to fight another day.

Temperamentally hot-headed and quickly irritated, Dragons will give as good as they get when angered, and do not display great sensitivity. They can be hypercritical if things aren't quite right, or not up their expectations.

Younger Dragons can lack self-confidence, but can too often swing the other way to become quite conceited and self-important, attracting enemies all too easily.

Generally, Dragons don't have to work at being liked - they are glamorous and magical, can light up gloomy moments and express a huge need to be loved.

FAMOUS DRAGONS

Lord Jeffrey Archer Author, politician	Former Prime Minister, musician, conductor, yachtsman
Geoffrey Boycott English cricket player, TV commentator	**HRH Prince Edward** Theatrical producer
Jimmy Connors International tennis champion	**Sir Yehudi Menuhin** Violinist, teacher
Kirk Douglas Film actor	**Zandra Rhodes** Fashion designer
Sir Edward Heath	**Ringo Starr** Drummer, singer, actor